LET'S LOOK AT Flowers

D1337002

Nicola Tuxworth

LORENZ BOOKS

Flowers everywhere

Flowers grow in all sorts of different places.

geranium

Indoor flowers

Some flowers will grow indoors.

thistle

dandelion

Wild flowers

Wild flowers grow in the countryside or on waste ground.

rose

pansy

Water flowers
Waterlilies
float on ponds
and lakes.

Garden flowers
Garden flowers
are grown in parks
and gardens.

cherry
blossom

**Flowers
on trees**
Some trees
flower in
the spring.

How do flowers grow?

Flowers need sunlight and air. They also need water, which they drink through their roots.

chrysanthemum

Sunlight

Sunlight helps plants to grow strong.

Rain

When it rains the soil gets wet. Flowers drink the water from the soil.

Colourful flowers

Flowers can be almost any colour. Which colours can you see?

deep purple
anemone
pink and
white lily
bright orange
chrysanthemums

Flowers all the year

Different flowers grow at different times of the year.

Spring flowers

daffodil

freesia

Summer flowers

sunflower

chrysanthemums

Autumn flowers

dahlia

scabious

Winter flower

winter pansy

Bursting into flower

Most flowers take a while to open.

The tulip flower is curled up inside this small bud.

Can you see the petals beginning to open? What colour are they?
Now the tulip flower is fully open. What colours can you see?
petal
stem

Seeds and bulbs

Some flowers grow from seeds. Others grow from bulbs.

golden tulip bulbs

wrinkled gladioli bulbs

smooth broad bean seeds

stripy sunflower seeds

hard sweetpea seeds

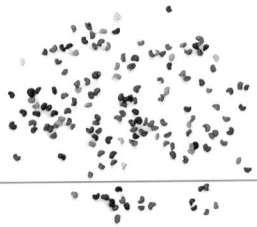

tiny poppy seeds

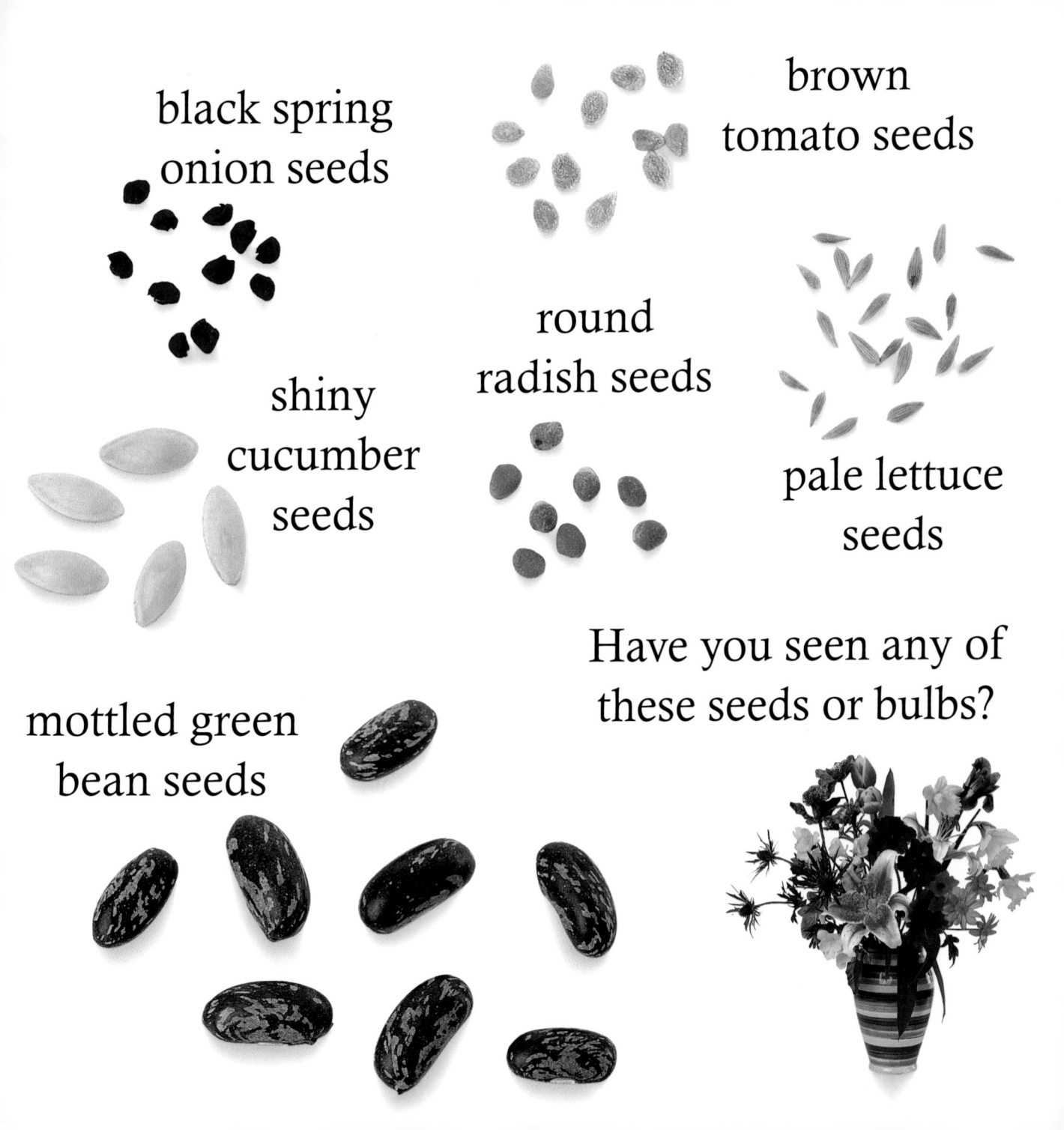
black spring onion seeds
brown tomato seeds
round radish seeds
shiny cucumber seeds
pale lettuce seeds
Have you seen any of these seeds or bulbs?
mottled green bean seeds

Flowers and food

Some flowers turn into fruit and vegetables for us to eat.

strawberry flowers

strawberries

apple blossom

pears

pear blossom

apples

runner bean flowers

runner beans

blackberry flowers and blackberries

marrow plant

marrow

Animal visitors

Birds, bees and butterflies all like to visit flowers.

Honey bees collect yellow pollen from flowers.

Some flowers turn into berries. The berries make a tasty feast for birds.

Butterflies like to sip the sweet juice inside flowers.

Growing flowers

You can grow flowers easily in a window box or a pot.

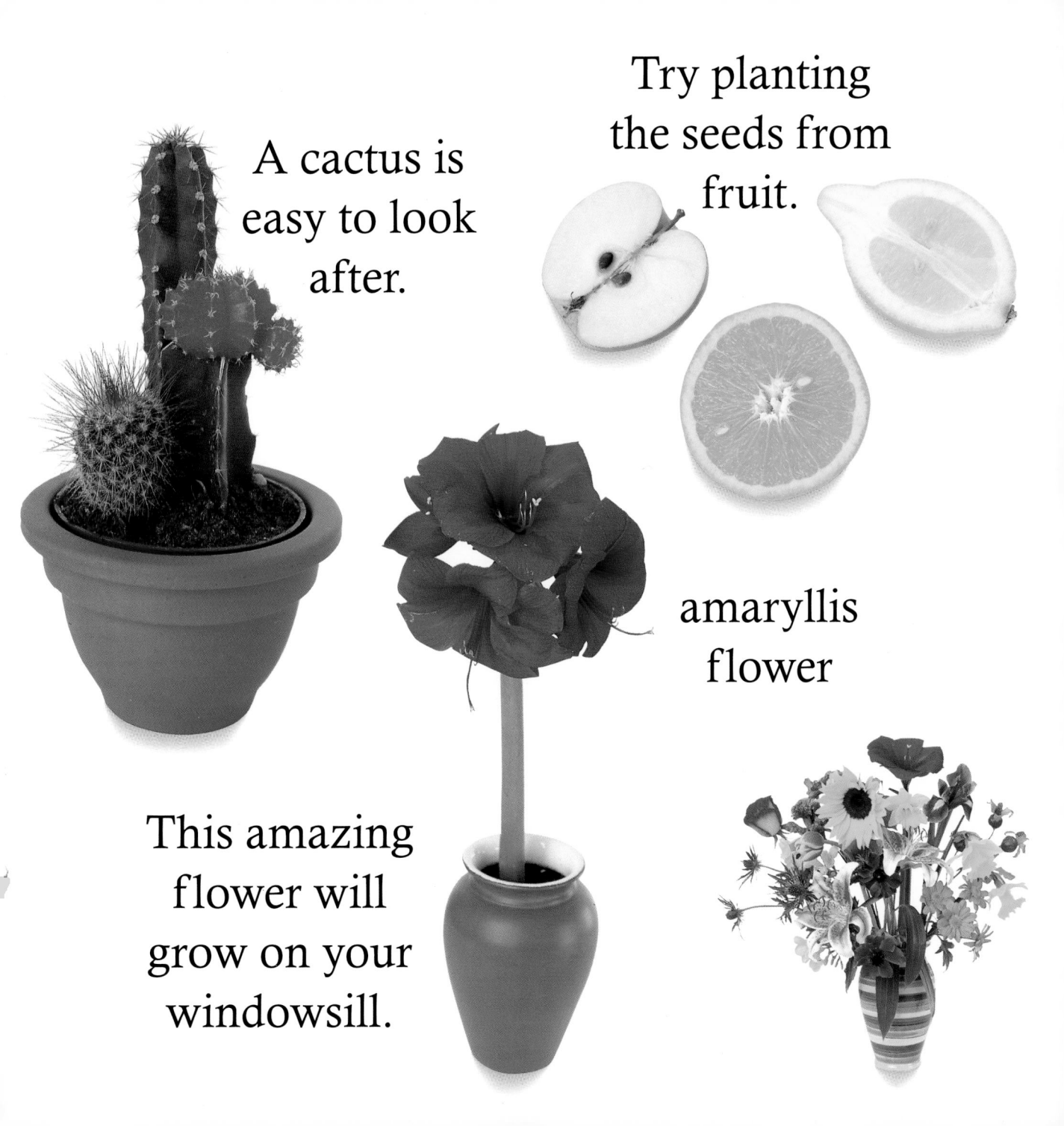
A cactus is easy to look after.
Try planting the seeds from fruit.
amaryllis flower
This amazing flower will grow on your windowsill.

Flowers for sale

Look at these roses. How many different colours can you see?